# CONNECTING THE DOTS: AN IN-DEPTH EXPLORATION OF NETWORKING FUNDAMENTALS.

2

# Contents

## Introduction

Title: The obvious conclusion is: A Top to bottom Gander at the Nuts and bolts of Systems administration In the huge universe of data innovation, organizing is the establishment, integrating the advanced web that makes up our cutting edge world. From the moment you connect to the internet to the seamless transfer of data between devices, networking is the silent force that propels our interconnected society forward. This careful helper hopes to unravel the complexities and demystify the phrasing incorporating frameworks organization, outfitting you with a solid preparation to investigate this strong space.

## Area 1: Layout of PC Associations

At its exemplification, a PC network is a plan of interconnected laptops and devices that talk with each other. These organizations arrive in different sizes and shapes, from little neighborhood arrangements in workplaces and homes to immense worldwide organizations that act as the web's establishment. The essential job of these associations is to work with the sharing of resources and information.

Inside the space of PC associations, there are three fundamental orders: Neighborhood (LANs), Wide Locale Associations (WANs), and Metropolitan District Associations (Screens). LANs cover a confined land district, similar to a single design or a grounds. Alternately,

WANs length greater distances, every now and again interacting LANs across metropolitan regions or even countries. Screens fall some in the center between, covering a city or a gigantic grounds.

## Second Section: Meaning of Frameworks organization nowadays

Sorting out expects a pressing part in our everyday schedules, driving the movement of information across the globe. The web, a goliath association of associations, has transformed into the groundwork of correspondence, exchange, and joint exertion. From sending messages to constant accounts, from partner by means of virtual diversion to getting to cloud-based organizations, every web based development is made possible through the convoluted snare of interconnected contraptions and structures.

Associations impact networks for reliable correspondence and useful sharing of resources. Medical services frameworks utilize organizations to smooth out quiet records and clinical data, and instructive foundations depend on them for e-learning. The importance of frameworks organization is furthermore featured by the presence of quick metropolitan networks, where interconnected devices overhaul metropolitan dwelling by smoothing out traffic stream, administering energy usage, and dealing with open organizations.

# Chapter Three: Basic Terminology

Before delving deeper into the concepts of systems administration, it is essential to grasp the following terminology:

Node: Any device related with an association, similar to computers, printers, or servers.

Router: A frameworks organization contraption that facilitates data traffic between different associations.

Switch: A contraption that interfaces various devices inside a local association, working with successful data exchange.

Hub: A more settled contraption that interfaces different devices anyway works at a lower level than a switch.

Modem: Short for modulator-demodulator, it changes over modernized signals from a PC into basic finishes paperwork for transmission over correspondence lines.

Passage: a gadget that utilizes Wi-Fi to interface remote gadgets to a wired organization.

## Part 4: Organizational Types

Understanding the various organizational types is essential for investigating the systems administration scene:

4.1 Neighborhood (LAN) LANs must be utilized in a little region, similar to a home, an office, or a grounds. They typically make use of Wi-Fi or Ethernet links to facilitate quick and efficient communication between devices within the same organization.

4.2 Wide District Association (WAN)
WANs cover greater geological locales and point of interaction various LANs. The actual web is a worldwide wide-region organization (WAN), making it

conceivable to move information between mainland's.

4.3 Metropolitan Region Organization (MAN) Monitors cover a city or a huge grounds and in the middle among LANs and WANs. They provide a network over a larger area than a LAN, but they are less flexible than a WAN.

4.4 Web versus Intranet
The web is an overall association that interfaces an immense number of public and secret associations all over the planet. Intranets, on the other hand, are private associations inside an affiliation, working with internal correspondence and resource sharing.

As we leave on this trip through the intricacies of frameworks organization, it's basic to see the fundamental work these different kinds of associations play in our interconnected world. Every association type fills a specific need, adding to the steady movement of information that portrays our electronic age.

**Kinds of Associations**

In the broad area of PC putting together, various kinds of associations fill different requirements, dealing with arranged needs and scales. Understanding these association types is fundamental to investigating the confounded snare of organization that describes our high level world.

## 1. Neighborhood (LAN):

An Area (LAN) is an association bound to a limited geographical district, similar to a lone construction, office, or grounds. LANs make it more straightforward for gadgets in a similar organization to impart rapidly and really. PCs, printers, and servers are instances of gadgets that are interconnected in a LAN through Ethernet links or remote associations. LANs are consistently used in homes, work environments, schools, and confidential endeavors.

## 2. Wide District Association (WAN):

A Wide Locale Association (WAN) ranges greater geological districts, interacting various LANs. WANs enable data move overextended isolates and are crucial for interconnecting networks across metropolitan networks, countries, or even expanses of land. The internet itself is the most extensive WAN, connecting millions of networks worldwide. WANs, which make use of leased lines, satellite links, optical fibers, and other technologies, enable communication over long distances.

## 3. Metropolitan District Association (MAN):

Geological inclusion places a Metropolitan Region Organization (MAN) between WANs and LANs. Covering a city or a huge grounds, Screens give network over a more prominent locale than a LAN yet are more restricted than a WAN. Multiple MANs are frequently connected by MANs within a metropolitan area. They expect a fundamental part in working with correspondence and resource giving for relationship to dissipated work environments inside a city.

## 4. Internet:

The Internet is the encapsulation of an overall Wide Locale Association (WAN). It interconnects endless public and secret associations all over the planet, enabling the exchanging of information on an overall scale. The web utilizes a blend of wired and far off developments, including fiber optics, satellite associations, and radio waves, to ensure steady correspondence across various locale.

## 5. Intranet:

While the web interfaces networks around the world, an Intranet is a classified association inside an affiliation. It serves as an internal close correspondence platform, enabling employees to collaborate on projects, share resources, and access company-specific data. Firewalls and other safety measures separate intranets from the public web.

## 6. Virtual Secret Association (VPN):

A secure online business network is known as a virtual confidential organization (VPN). Users can access a private network from a distance, just like they would if they were there. VPNs are consistently used for secure distant permission to corporate associations or for ensuring the assurance and security of data conveyed over open associations.

## 7. Individual District Association (Compartment):

An individual region organization, otherwise called a "Dish," is a little organization that interfaces gadgets that are inside a couple of meters of a person. Bluetooth and infrared affiliations are examples of headways used in Holder to associate devices like PDAs, computers, and wearable contraptions.

## 8. Grounds Locale Association (CAN):

The purpose of a Grounds Region Organization (CAN) is to connect networks within a limited geological area, such as a college campus or modern complex. Jars provide a quick network between the grounds' various offices and structures, facilitating productive correspondence and asset sharing.

Understanding these various kinds of associations gives a foundation to comprehending the complexities of current organization. Whether it's the close by collaborations inside a LAN or the overall exchanges worked with by the web, each kind of association expects an unquestionable part in shaping how we give and offer information in our interconnected world.

## jOrganizing Gadgets: Exploring the Trap of Network

In the mind boggling scene of PC organizing, a large number of gadgets cooperate flawlessly to empower correspondence and information move. These gadgets act as the structure blocks of interconnected networks, going from little neighborhood arrangements to tremendous worldwide foundations. Understanding the jobs and elements of these systems administration gadgets is fundamental for anybody digging into the universe of network.

## 1. Router:

The switch remains as a crucial gadget in any organization, liable for coordinating information traffic between various organizations.

Switches work at the organization layer (Layer 3) of the OSI model and settle on choices in view of IP addresses. They interface numerous organizations, empowering information parcels to productively track down their direction from source to objective. In home organizations, a switch frequently joins the functionalities of a switch, switch, and remote passageway.

## 2. Switch:

A switch works at the information interface layer (Layer 2) and is intended to interface numerous gadgets inside a nearby organization. Not at all like a center, which communicates information to every associated gadget, a switch wisely advances information just to the particular gadget that needs it.

This improves the proficiency of information move inside a Neighborhood (LAN) by lessening pointless traffic.

### 3. Hub:

While more uncommon in current organizations, a center point is a straightforward systems administration gadget that interfaces different gadgets inside a LAN. Centers work at the actual layer (Layer 1) and broadcast information to every associated gadget, prompting more organization blockage contrasted with switches. Because of their restricted knowledge, centers have to a great extent been supplanted by additional effective switches.

## 4. Modem:

The expression "modem" is gotten from "modulator-demodulator," featuring its job in changing over computerized signals from a PC into simple signs for transmission over correspondence lines, as well as the other way around. Modems are significant for interfacing with the web, whether through conventional telephone lines (DSL) or fast link associations.

## 5. Passage:

A Passageway (AP) is a gadget that permits remote empowered gadgets to interface with a wired organization utilizing Wi-Fi. As the link between wired and wireless communication, access points are essential components of wireless networks. They empower the production of remote

Neighborhood (WLANs) by working with associations between gadgets like PCs, cell phones, and tablets.

## 6. Repeater:

In the domain of remote organizations, a repeater assumes a fundamental part in broadening the scope of a Wi-Fi signal. It gets the remote sign, enhances it, and retransmits it, really extending the inclusion region. Repeaters are helpful in defeating hindrances or distance-related signal constriction, guaranteeing a more hearty remote organization.

## 7. Firewall:

A firewall fills in as a defensive boundary between a confidential organization and the web, observing and controlling approaching and active organization traffic in light of foreordained security rules. Firewalls are essential for protecting organizations against unapproved access, digital dangers, and pernicious exercises. They can be carried out as equipment gadgets or programming applications.

## 8. Changing Hub:

An exchanging center consolidates the functionalities of a customary center point and a switch. It works at both the actual layer (Layer 1) and the information interface layer (Layer 2), taking into consideration effective information move inside an organization. A switching hub may not offer the same level of intelligence and control as a dedicated switch, despite being more intelligent than a hub.

### 9. Bridge:

A scaffold interfaces and channels traffic between at least two organization fragments at the information connect layer (Layer 2). Spans are utilized to upgrade network execution by lessening pointless traffic and disconnecting issues inside unambiguous sections.

These systems administration gadgets, each with its special reason and usefulness, structure the foundation of present day correspondence. From switches guiding information across the web to switches guaranteeing productive correspondence inside a neighborhood organization, these gadgets team up to make the mind boggling trap of network that characterizes our computerized age. Understanding their jobs is fundamental for anybody looking to explore the intricacies of PC organizing.

## Organizing Conventions: The Language of Availability

In the tremendous scene of PC organizing, conventions act as the fundamental dialects that empower gadgets to consistently convey and share data. The manner in which data is sent, received, and interpreted across networks is governed by these standard sets of rules. Understanding the key systems administration conventions is pivotal for building a strong groundwork in the realm of network.

## 1. Suite of TCP/IP protocols:

It comprises of a set-up of correspondence conventions that empower gadgets to interface and trade information across networks. TCP gives dependable, association situated correspondence, while IP handles the tending to and steering of information bundles. The TCP/IP suite incorporates conventions like HTTP, FTP, and DNS, which are essential to web correspondence.

## 2. HTTP/HTTPS:

HTTP (Hypertext Move Convention) and its safe partner HTTPS (Hypertext Move Convention Secure) are application layer conventions utilized for sending hypertext archives on the Internet. HTTP characterizes how messages are organized and sent, while HTTPS adds a layer of encryption to get information move, making it fundamental for secure internet based exchanges.

## 3. FTP (Document Move Convention):

The Record Move Convention (FTP) is a standard organization convention utilized for moving documents between a client and a server on a PC organization. FTP works on a client-server model, permitting clients to transfer or download documents effortlessly. It is ordinarily utilized for overseeing site content, programming appropriation, and record sharing.

## 4. DNS (Space Name Framework):

The Space Name Framework (DNS) is a various leveled decentralized naming framework that interprets comprehensible area names into mathematical IP addresses. DNS assumes an essential part in working with easy to use web perusing by empowering clients to get to sites utilizing space names as opposed to recollecting complex IP addresses.

## 5. DHCP (Dynamic Host Setup Convention):

Dynamic Host Setup Convention (DHCP) is an organization convention used to naturally dole out IP addresses and other organization design data to gadgets on an organization. DHCP improves on network organization by powerfully dispensing and overseeing IP addresses, guaranteeing effective utilization of accessible assets.

## 6. Simple Mail Transfer Protocol, or SMTP:

The Straightforward Mail Move Convention (SMTP) is an application layer convention for electronic mail transmission. It characterizes the principles for sending messages between servers. SMTP is central to email correspondence, taking into account the solid conveyance of messages across various mail servers.

**7. POP3/IMAP (Mailing station Convention 3/Web Message Access Convention):**

POP3 (Mail center Convention 3) and IMAP (Web Message Access Convention) are email recovery conventions. POP3 downloads messages from a server to a client gadget, while IMAP permits clients to see and control messages straightforwardly on the server. These conventions oversee how email clients cooperate with mail servers.

**8. TCP and UDP (Transmission Control Convention and Client Datagram Convention):**

TCP and UDP are transport layer conventions inside the TCP/IP suite, giving different correspondence draws near. TCP offers dependable, association arranged correspondence, guaranteeing that information is conveyed precisely and properly aligned. On the other hand, UDP does not require a connection and is frequently utilized in real-time applications where a minimal amount of data loss is tolerated.

## 9. ICMP (Web Control Message Convention):

The Web Control Message Convention (ICMP) is a fundamental piece of the Web Convention (IP). It is basically utilized for demonstrative purposes and blunder announcing in network correspondence. ICMP incorporates capabilities like ping, which tests the reach ability of a host on a web convention organization.

## 10. Simple Network Management Protocol, or SNMP,:

Straightforward Organization The board Convention (SNMP) is an application layer convention used to oversee and screen network gadgets. Device information can be gathered, network performance can be monitored, and device behavior can be controlled with SNMP.

Learning the languages spoken by the devices that power the internet and other computer networks is comparable to mastering these networking protocols. Whether working with web perusing, email correspondence, or record moves, these conventions structure the foundation of a normalized and interconnected computerized world, guaranteeing consistent correspondence across different gadgets and organizations.

**Submitting and IP areas:**

Examining the Watching out for Scene In the enormous universe of PC affiliation, IP normally goes probably as the general direction that grant contraptions to find and talk with one another. Arranging able and framed networks requires a fundamental view of IP tending and subnetting. This evaluation skips into the basics of IP addresses, their sorts, and the specialty of subnetting.

## 1. IPv4 versus IPv6:

1.1 IPv4: Structure 4 of the Web Show

The Internet Show type that is utilized the most frequently is IPv4. It makes use of a 32-cycle address plot, also known as four plans of numbers restricted by spots (like 192.168.0.1, for example). By virtue of the set number of IPv4 tends to open, IPv6 has been embraced.

1.2 Construction 6 of the Web Show (IPv6):

By introducing a 128-cycle address plot, IPv6 is needed to address the depletion of IPv4 addresses. Eight parties of hexadecimal numbers separated by colons are used to create IPv6 addresses (f or example, 2001:0db8:85a3:0000:0000:8a2e:0 370:7334). IPv6 ensures the web's happened with extension by giving inestimable express locales.

## 2. IP Address Classes:

IP typically falls into one of five categories: A, B, C, D, and E are the classes that tend to networks the most often. 2.1 A-Level:

Reasonable for huge association with a crucial number of hosts.

2.2 Class B:

Range: Default Subnet Cover: 128.0.0.0 to 191.255.255.255 For associations of medium size, 255.255.0.0 is appropriate.

2.3 Class C:

3. Subnetting Essentials:

What definitively is subnetting? Subnetting is the strategy drawn in with confining a more undeniable relationship into extra unpretentious, more sensible sub-affiliations or subnets. It maintains network productivity by reducing transmission districts and increasing asset utilization.

3.2 Subnet Security:

A subnet cover is a 32-digit numeric locale that limits an IP address into association and host parts. It is tended to in spotted decimal association, concurring with the IP address.

3.3 Subnetting Model:
Consider the IP address 192.168.1.0 with the default Class C subnet cover 255.255.255.0. By subnetting, you can detach it into more subtle subnets, each with its degree of usable addresses. For example:

Crude Between Region Figuring out (CIDR) documentation pays special attention to IP addresses and their connected organizing prefix. It is given as IP_address/prefix_length and takes into account a piece of IP that is more adaptable (for example, 192.168.1.0/24).

4. Private and Public IP Regions:
4.1 Dumbfounding IP addresses:

## 4.2 Areas of public IP:

Public IP addresses are generally speaking perfect and routable on the web. They are delegated by Organization access Providers (ISPs) and ought to stand separated on every device related with the public web.

## 5. IPv6 Subnetting:

IPv6 subnetting keeps equivalent rules to IPv4 yet with the genuinely extensive area space. In CIDR documentation, subnetting is normally portrayed as 2001: db8::/48.

Sensible connection plan and the managers start with an impression of IP addresses and subnetting. Whether isolating colossal relationship into sensible divides or designating addresses for unequivocal purposes, IP tending to and subnetting structure the supporting of worked with and convincing correspondence in the modernized age.

## Organizing Models: Disentangling the Layers of Network

In the powerful universe of PC organizing, models act as outlines, giving an organized structure to understanding how various components cooperate to work with correspondence. Two noticeable systems administration models — the OSI (Open Frameworks Interconnection) model and the TCP/IP (Transmission Control Convention/Web Convention) model — guide the plan and usefulness of present day organizations. We should investigate these models and their importance in molding the network scene.

## 1. OSI Model:

The OSI model is a calculated structure that normalizes the elements of a telecom or figuring framework into seven particular layers. Each layer plays a particular part, and the model guarantees that gadgets from various makers can flawlessly impart.

## 1.1 Physical Layer, or First Layer:

The actual layer manages the actual association between gadgets. It specifies cables, connectors, and the physical medium for the transmission of raw binary data.

## 1.2 Second Data Link Layer:

The information interface layer is liable for making a solid connection between two straightforwardly associated hubs. It organizes data into packets, controls access to the physical medium, and guarantees error-free communication within the local network.

## 1.3 Organization Layer (Layer 3):

Data routing and forwarding between devices on various networks is the primary focus of the network layer. It allocates sensible addresses (IP addresses) to gadgets and decides the best way for information transmission.

## 1.4 Vehicle Layer (Layer 4):

The vehicle layer guarantees start to finish correspondence and unwavering quality. It oversees stream control, blunder rectification, and information division, isolating enormous messages into more modest sections for proficient transmission.

## 1.5 Meeting Layer (Layer 5):

The meeting layer lays out, keeps up with, and ends meetings or associations between applications. It manages dialog control, making it possible for applications running on different devices to exchange data.

## 1.6 Show Layer (Layer 6):

Encryption and data translation are the primary focuses of the presentation layer. It guarantees that information is introduced in a clear configuration for the application layer and handles errands like pressure and encryption.

## 1.7 The Application Layer:

The interface between the user and the network is the application layer. It gives network benefits straightforwardly to end-clients and applications, working with assignments like record moves, email, and remote login.

## 2. TCP/IP Model:

The TCP/IP model is a compact, four-layer system that mirrors the design of the conventions that power the web. It has turned into the true norm for current systems administration.

### 2.1 Connection Layer (or Organization Point of interaction Layer):

The TCP/IP link layer is in charge of the physical connection and local network communication, just like the OSI data link layer. It incorporates the sensible connection control (LLC) and media access control (Macintosh) sub-layers.

## 2.2 Web Layer:

Identical to the OSI network layer, the web layer oversees coherent tending to, steering, and fracture of information parcels. It is where the Web Convention (IP) works.

## 2.3 Layer of Transport:

Matching the OSI transport layer, the TCP/IP transport layer guarantees dependable start to finish correspondence. It incorporates both the Transmission Control Convention (TCP) for association situated correspondence and the Client Datagram Convention (UDP) for connectionless correspondence.

## 2.4 Application Layer:

In the TCP/IP model, the application layer envelops

functionalities from the OSI application, show, and meeting layers. It gives network benefits straightforwardly to end-clients and applications, supporting undertakings like email, record moves, and remote access.

### 3. Correlation of OSI and TCP/IP Models:

While the OSI model gives an exhaustive structure, the TCP/IP model is more smoothed out and intently lines up with the conventions driving the web. The TCP/IP model is frequently preferred for its common sense and direct significance to genuine world systems administration situations.

Understanding these models is essential for network specialists and directors, offering a reasonable structure to investigate issues, plan organizations, and guarantee interoperability between various systems administration innovations. Whether exploring the seven-layered progressive system of the OSI model or embracing the common sense of the four-layered TCP/IP model, these structures are key instruments for building and keeping up with the interconnected world we depend on today.

## Getting the Organization:

Safeguarding the Computerized Wilderness In when information is the backbone of the two organizations and people, network security fills in as a guard dog, making preparations for a plenty of dangers that could imperil data's respectability, privacy, and accessibility. This examination jumps into the fundamentals of association security, typical risks, and the frameworks used to reinforce progressed scenes.

## 1. Firewalls: The Automated Watchmen

Firewalls go probably as the fundamental line of assurance, noticing and controlling drawing nearer and dynamic association traffic considering destined security rules. They can be executed as gear machines or programming applications and expect a fundamental part in preventing unapproved permission to associations and contraptions.

## 2. Encryption: Getting the High level Conversations

Encryption changes significant data into a coded plan, conveying it garbled without the reasonable unscrambling key. This ensures the protection of delicate information, making it a central piece of secure correspondence over networks. Shows like SSL/TLS encode data sent over the web, guaranteeing secure trades.

## 3. Virtual Secret Associations (VPNs):

Virtual Confidential Organizations (VPNs) give clients safe admittance to private organizations by making scrambled burrows over the web. VPNs are typically used to ensure privacy and security, particularly when communicating remotely with corporate organizations or accessing sensitive data over open networks.

## 4. Typical Security Risks: The High level Adversaries

4.1 Malware: Threats to network security include ransomware, trojan horses, viruses, and other forms of malware. These pernicious programming components can attack structures, compromise data, and upset commonplace exercises.

4.2 Defrauding: Misleading Computerized Methods Phishing entails tricking people into discovering sensitive data by posing as a trustworthy substance. Phishing attacks oftentimes come as interesting messages, destinations, or messages, zeroing in on confused clients.

4.3 Conveyed Disavowal of Administration (DDoS) and Forswearing of Administration (DoS): Overwhelming Attacks DoS attacks make a business or administration inaccessible to customers by flooding it with traffic. DDoS attacks increase this risk by arranging attacks from various sources meanwhile, overwhelming the assigned system.

4.4 The Middle Man: Man-in-the-Center Attacks necessitate capturing and possibly altering correspondence between two parties. Attackers can tune in on delicate information or implant poisonous substance into the correspondence stream.

## 5. Security Best Practices: Supporting the High level Fortress

5.1 Access Control: Limiting Passage Utilizing hearty access controls guarantees that particular assets are open just to approved clients. This incorporates the usage of secure confirmation strategies, work based induction controls, and intermittent audits to screen client works out.

5.2 Standard Programming Updates: Advanced Protection Fixing Programming, working frameworks, and applications that could be taken advantage of by aggressors should be regularly refreshed. Typical updates redesign security and defend against known risks.

5.3 Association Noticing: Watchfulness, all things considered Reliable association noticing considers the revelation of astonishing activities or potential security breaks.

5.4 Security Getting ready and Care: Empowering the Human Firewall Training clients about security risks and best practices is principal. Human misstep is a common justification behind security episodes, and care planning can empower individuals to see and avoid likely risks.

## 6. Emerging Developments: The Destiny of Association Security

6.1 Zero Trust Designing: Trust No one, Really take a look at Everything

Zero Trust is a creating security model that anticipates no substance, whether inside or outside the association, can be depended upon as per usual. It orders incessant affirmation of the character and security position of all clients and contraptions.

6.2 Artificial intelligence (AI) and man-made consciousness (computer-based intelligence): Vigilant Gatekeeper

Recreated insight and ML are logically utilized for risk disclosure and assessment, working on the ability to ceaselessly perceive and answer security events. These advancements can dissect examples and behavior patterns to anticipate and avert potential dangers.

6.3 Blockchain in Organization security: The use of blockchain technology is being investigated as a means of safeguarding digital transactions and enhancing data integrity. Unchanging security Its decentralized and modify safe nature offers new streets for ensuring the authenticity and dependability of information.

Defenders of computerized scenes are resolutely bracing themselves against a continuously expanding cluster of threats, making network security a never-ending waiting game. By joining overwhelming mechanical plans, best practices, and ceaseless preparation, the high level edges can be investigated securely, ensuring that associations stay solid even with emerging hardships.

## Administration of remote systems: Communicating Without Limits

Far off frameworks organization has changed how we partner contraptions, engaging correspondence without the constraints of genuine connections. This examination jumps into the nuts and bolts of far off frameworks organization, the advances driving it, and the considerations essential for laying out secure and useful remote circumstances.

### 1. Innovations Offline:

1.1 Remote Constancy, or Wi-Fi:
Wi-Fi is an inescapable far off development that licenses contraptions to communicate with an area (LAN) from a distance. It

works considering the IEEE 802.11 gathering of standards, giving high speed web access in homes, associations, and public spaces. Information is sent among gadgets and passages through Wi-Fi utilizing radio recurrence signals.

1.2 Bluetooth:
It works in the 2.4 GHz repeat range and is known for its low power usage, making it ideal for individual district associations (Dish).

1.3 NFC (Near Handle Correspondence):
Short-range correspondence between gadgets, commonly inside a couple of centimeters, is made conceivable by NFC. It is typically used for tagging, data transfer between devices, and contactless payments.

## 2. Wi-Fi Instructions:

2.1 802.11a/b/g/n/ac/ax:

The 802.11 gathering of rules incorporates various times of Wi-Fi development:

802.11a/b/g: presented in the middle of the 2000s, with various recurrence groups and information rates.

802.11n: Introduced in 2009, offering additionally created speed and reach.

802.11ac: Introduced in 2013, giving speedier velocities and further developed execution in the 5 GHz repeat band.

802.11ax (Wi-Fi 6): The latest standard beginning around my last update in 2022, expected to augment efficiency in predicament pressed conditions and sponsorship more simultaneous affiliations.

### 3. Distant Association Parts:

## 3.1 Far off Paths (WAPs):

Far off Entries go about as the central community focuses for Wi-Fi associations. They engage contraptions to communicate from a distance to the wired association system. In greater associations, various paths structure a distant association to give predictable consideration.

## 3.2 Remote Switches:

Remote Switches join the functionalities of a standard switch with those of a distant entry. They regulate network traffic, give out IP locations, and give Wi-Fi accessibility, making them ordinary in homes and confidential endeavors.

3.3 Distant Association Connectors:
Distant Association Connectors are contraptions that grant computers and various devices to interact with a far off association. They can be composed into devices (e.g., workstations) or added from a distance (e.g., USB connectors).

## 4. Considerations for Remote Security:

4.1 WPA3 (Wi-Fi Protected Induction 3):
The most recent Wi-Fi security standard, WPA3, provides more solid encryption and protection against typical attacks. It further develops Wi-Fi security,

particularly in home and undertaking conditions.

## 4.2 SSID (Organization Set Identifier) Broadcasting:

Crippling SSID broadcasting can add a layer of wellbeing by making the association less recognizable to anticipated attackers. Regardless, it's just a single piece of wellbeing and should be used connected with various measures.

## 4.3 Encryption Shows:

At the point when information is sent over a remote organization, solid encryption conventions like WPA3-AES (High level Encryption Standard) guarantee that it stays private and secure.

## 5. Hardships and Courses of action:

## 5.1 Interruption:

Far off associations can stand up to impedance from other electronic devices, bordering Wi-Fi associations, or genuine obstacles. Using double band switches, picking the right channels, and using signal promoters are all examples of arrangements.

## 5.2 Security Concerns:

Security is a basic concern in distant associations. Using strong encryption, reliably invigorating passwords, and engaging organization security features are central measures to lighten security possibilities.

## 5.3 Degree and Inclusion:

Far off association consideration can be affected by the size of the space and real limits. Extending consideration can be achieved by unequivocally setting paths, using repeaters, or sending network associations.

## 6. Future Examples:

### 6.1 Wi-Fi 6E and 5G:

The joining of 5G cell advancement and the introduction of Wi-Fi 6E (contacted the 6 GHz repeat band) are shaping the possible destiny of remote organization. These headways ensure speedier velocities, lower lethargy, and extended limit concerning extra related contraptions.

### 6.2 Web of Things, or IoT:

The increase of IoT contraptions adds to the creating interest for useful and secure far off associations. Later on, remote innovations should have the option to meet the different correspondence necessities of many associated gadgets.

Far off frameworks organization has progressed into an essential piece of our everyday schedules, giving the versatility and solace of organization without genuine goals. The scene of remote systems administration will without a doubt see extra developments as innovation progresses, guaranteeing that our computerized communications keep on being secure and consistent.

## Basics of Troubleshooting: Exploring the Organization Difficulties

Investigating is a fundamental ability for anybody engaged with overseeing PC organizations. It includes distinguishing, disconnecting, and settling issues to guarantee the smooth activity of organized frameworks. This guide covers the fundamentals of organization investigating, giving an organized way to deal with address normal difficulties.

### 1. Characterize the Issue:

### 1.1 Complaints by Users:

Begin by social affair data about client revealed issues. Obviously characterize the issue by asking clients for explicit subtleties, for example, blunder messages, the recurrence of events, and the impacted gadgets or applications.

1.2 Symptoms and Observations:
Make your own observations to find the problem's symptoms. Search for designs, blunder messages, or surprising ways of behaving that can assist with pinpointing the issue.

2. Disengage the Issue:
2.1 Client or Framework explicit:
Determine whether the issue affects just one user or device. In the event that different clients are impacted, the issue might be fundamental.

2.2 Local or network:
Separate between far reaching issues and those restricted to a

particular neighborhood. This aides in deciding the extent of the issue.

## 2.3 Physical or Intelligent:

Recognize actual layer (equipment) and coherent layer (programming, design) issues. Knowing the layer of the OSI model where the issue lies helps with focused on investigating.

## 3. Accumulate Data:

### 3.1 Organization Geography:

Comprehend the organization geography to distinguish possible weak spots. Map out the organization parts, including switches, switches, and passages.

### 3.2 Documentation and logs:

Check framework logs, blunder messages, and documentation for any pertinent data. Historical data can shed light on persistent problems.

### 3.3 User Comments:

Draw in with clients to accumulate extra data. Inquire about any recent updates, modifications, or unusual behavior they may have observed.

## 4. Use Organization Investigating Apparatuses:

### 4.1 Ping:

To check for basic connectivity between devices, use the ping command. It checks in the event that a gadget can arrive at one more gadget on the organization.

### 4.2 Traceroute/Tracepath:

Using traceroute (Windows) or tracepath (Linux), an issue can be identified at the hop where data packets travel to a destination.

4.3 Analyzers of the Network:
Devices like Wireshark catch and dissect network traffic, giving nitty gritty experiences into the bundles crossing the organization. Anomalies and errors can be discovered by analyzing packet captures.

4.4 IP Arrangement:
Check IP arrangements utilizing orders like ipconfig (Windows) or ifconfig (Linux) to guarantee gadgets have right IP addresses, subnet veils, and passages.

## 5. Check Network and Conventions:

### 5.1 Actually look at Actual Associations:

Make certain that all cables, connectors, and physical connections are intact. A free link or defective connector can prompt network issues.

### 5.2 Convention Arrangements:

Check that network conventions (TCP/IP settings, DHCP, DNS) are accurately designed. Wrong settings can bring about correspondence disappointments.

## 6. Check Safety efforts:

### 6.1 Firewall and Security Programming:

Examine the configurations of security software and the firewall settings. Firewalls can hinder genuine traffic, and misconfigurations might bring about correspondence issues.

## 6.2 Controls for Access:

Check access control records (upper leg tendons) and authorizations to guarantee that clients and gadgets have the vital freedoms to get to assets.

## 7. Make adjustments with caution:

### 7.1 Rollback Plan:

Prior to carrying out changes, have a rollback plan in the event that the progressions demolish what is happening. This guarantees that you can return to the past state rapidly.

### 7.2 Change Control Systems:

Stick to change control systems, particularly in big business conditions. Record changes, impart them to significant partners, and timetable changes during low-influence periods if conceivable.

## 8. Seek Extra Assistance:

### 8.1 Counsel Documentation and Online Assets:

Use online resources and documentation that are specific to the hardware, software, or problem at hand. Community forums and documentation from vendors can be useful sources of information.

### 8.2 Work together with Friends:

To get help, get involved with colleagues or online communities. Cooperative critical thinking frequently brings new viewpoints and experiences.

## 9. Raise When Essential:

### 9.1 Distinguish When to Raise:

On the off chance that the issue continues or on the other hand assuming it includes basic frameworks, heighten the issue to more elevated level help, framework executives, or seller support.

### 9.2 Record Goals:

Report the means taken and the goal for future reference. This forms an information base and helps in investigating comparative issues.

## 10. Preventive Measures:

### 10.1 Ordinary Upkeep:

Updates, patches, and backups are all regular maintenance tasks that can be done to prevent problems before they happen.

### 10.2 Preparation and Mindfulness:

Put resources into preparing for network executives and end-clients to improve attention to security rehearses and decrease the probability of issues.

Network investigating is a dynamic and iterative cycle that requires a precise methodology and flexibility. By following these investigating rudiments, network experts can proficiently distinguish and determine issues, guaranteeing the ceaseless and secure activity of PC organizations.

**Distributed computing and Systems administration: Crossing over the Computerized Skyline**

Distributed computing has changed the scene of IT framework, offering versatile, on-request assets and administrations over the web. Organizing assumes a vital part in associating clients, applications, and information to cloud administrations. This investigation digs into the harmonious connection between distributed computing and systems administration, itemizing key ideas, structures, and contemplations.

**1. Distributed computing Basics:**

**1.1 Assistance Models:**

IaaS, or infrastructure as a service, is Gives virtualized processing assets over the web, permitting clients to send and oversee virtual machines, stockpiling, and organizations.

PaaS, or Platform as a Service, is Offers a stage permitting engineers to fabricate, send, and oversee applications without managing the basic framework.

Programming as a Help (SaaS): Conveys programming applications over the web, dispensing with the requirement for neighborhood establishments and upkeep.

1.2 Organization Models:

Cloud Public: Administrations are given over the web and accessible to the overall population.

Confidential Cloud: Foundation is only utilized by a solitary association.

Crossover Cloud: Coordinates both public and confidential mists, permitting information and applications to be divided among them.

## 2. Essentials of Cloud Networking:

### 2.1 Virtual Confidential Cloud (VPC):

Openly mists, a Virtual Confidential Cloud (VPC) gives a coherently disengaged part of the cloud where clients can send off assets.

It permits customization of the organization design, including IP address range, subnets, and directing tables.

### 2.2 Burden Adjusting:

Load balancers disseminate approaching organization traffic across different servers to guarantee no single server is overpowered, improving unwavering quality and accessibility.

## 2.3 Substance Conveyance Organizations (CDNs):

CDNs upgrade the conveyance of web content by storing it on servers found decisively all over the planet, diminishing dormancy and further developing execution.

## 3. Interfacing with the Cloud:

### 3.1 Virtual Confidential Organizations (VPNs):

VPNs lay out secure associations between an association's on-premises organization and the cloud, empowering secure information move over the web.

### 3.2 Direct Interface:

Direct Associate gives devoted, confidential organization associations between on-premises server farms and cloud suppliers, bypassing the public web for improved security and unwavering quality.

## 4. Security in Cloud Systems administration:

4.1 Shared Liability Model:

Users are accountable for security "in" the cloud, which includes data, applications, and access controls, according to a shared responsibility model followed by cloud providers.

4.2 Personality and Access The board (IAM):

Control access to cloud resources with robust IAM policies to make sure that only authorized services and users can interact with sensitive data.

4.3 Security:

Use encryption for information very still, on the way, and during handling. Overall security can be improved by using tools like AWS

Key Management Service (KMS) to encrypt data and use SSL/TLS for communication.

**5. Adaptability and Versatility:**

5.1 Auto-scaling:

Influence auto-scaling to naturally change the quantity of process assets in view of interest. This guarantees ideal execution during busy times and cost reserve funds during low interest.

5.2 Flexible Burden Adjusting:

Flexible Burden Adjusting (ELB) benefits consequently circulate approaching application traffic across numerous objectives, adjusting to changes in application interest.

## 6. DevOps and Cloud Systems administration:

6.1 Framework as Code (IaC):
Automating the provisioning and management of cloud resources, such as Terraform or AWS CloudFormation, ensures consistency and efficiency.

6.2 Persistent Reconciliation/Consistent Sending (CI/Cd):
Execute CI/Album pipelines to mechanize the testing and arrangement of uses in the cloud, diminishing manual mediation and speeding up discharge cycles.

## 7. Observing and Streamlining:

7.1 Tools for Cloud Monitoring:
Use cloud-local checking apparatuses like Amazon CloudWatch or Google Cloud Observing to acquire bits of

knowledge into the exhibition and soundness of cloud assets.

7.2 Expense The executives:

Consistently survey and streamline cloud costs by right-estimating examples, utilizing saved cases, and observing asset utilization to wipe out pointless costs.

## 8. Cloud Networking and Edge Computing:

8.1 Edge Areas:

Edge figuring finishes registering assets closer clients by putting servers in edge areas. This decreases dormancy and works on the responsiveness of utilizations.

8.2 IoT Joining:

Cloud organizing assumes an imperative part in supporting Web of Things (IoT) organizations, working with the association of gadgets to cloud administrations for information handling and examination.

## 9. Difficulties and Contemplations:

### 9.1 Information Move Expenses:

Be aware of information move costs, particularly in situations including huge volumes of information moving .

## Emerging Developments: Framing What was in store Electronic Scene

The development scene is incessantly creating, driven by progression and the mission for capability, accessibility, and redesigned capacities. Emerging advances are at the front of this turn of events, promising notable changes across various undertakings. This study examines some of the most important emerging innovations that are poised to shape the future.

### 1. Man-made intellectual prowess (PC based knowledge) and simulated intelligence (ML):

1.1 man-made knowledge in Computerization:

Recreated insight driven automation is modifying adventures by streamlining processes, reducing expenses, and chipping away at all around viability. From mechanical cycle motorization (RPA) to shrewd unique systems, man-made knowledge is a central purpose.

1.2 Involving ML in Prescient Examination:

Computer based intelligence estimations look at tremendous datasets to recognize models, examples, and associations. This enables associations to make data driven figures and decisions, redesigning orchestrating and resource apportioning.

## 2. 5G Advancement:

## 2.1 Quick Organization:

5G development offers on a very basic level speedier web rates and lower inertia diverged from its precursors. It supports applications like expanded reality and computer generated reality, maintains the Web of Things (IoT), and works with ongoing correspondence.

## 2.2 Edge Enrolling Blend:

The blend of 5G and edge figuring reduces data dealing with time via conveying enrolling resources closer to the wellspring of data. This is fundamental for applications requiring low dormancy, similar to autonomous vehicles and splendid metropolitan networks.

## 3. Blockchain and Decentralized Advances:

### 3.1 Blockchain for Security:

Blockchain development ensures secure, clear, and modify safe trades. Past cryptographic cash, it finds applications in store network the leaders, clinical consideration, and high level character affirmation.

### 3.2 Clever Contracts:

Splendid arrangements, self-executing contracts with the terms directly made into code, modernize and carry out definitive game plans. They make it easier to understand and get better at different things.

## 4. IoT (Web of Things):

### 4.1 Related Devices:

This accessibility engages data collection, remote noticing, and robotization across undertakings like clinical consideration, cultivation, and splendid homes.

4.2 Dangers to IoT Security:

As the amount of related contraptions grows, so do stresses over security. To defend delicate information and forestall unapproved access, it is vital for execute hearty safety efforts for IoT gadgets.

AR and VR progresses make distinctive experiences in gaming, tutoring, planning, and virtual participation. The fields of design, diversion, and medical care all advantage from these innovations.

## 5. Mixed Reality (MR):

Blended Reality combines elements from both the real and virtual worlds, allowing users to gradually connect with advanced content. This development is progressing for applications in plan, gathering, and tutoring.

## 6. Biotechnology and Genomics:

6.1 CRISPR Development:

CRISPR (Grouped Regularly Interspaced Short Palindromic Repeats) is major areas of strength for a modifying gadget with applications in genetic assessment, disease treatment, and conceivably redirecting genetic issues.

6.2 Clinical Accuracy:

Exactness drug tailors clinical medications to individual credits, considering factors like inherited characteristics, lifestyle, and environment. It aims to reduce adverse effects and increase treatment adequacy.

## 7. Quantum Figuring:

### 7.1 Quantum Supreme quality:

Quantum laptops impact quantum bits (qubits) to perform complex computations at speeds unfathomable for outdated laptops. Quantum uniqueness tends to the accomplishment where quantum computers beat the capacities of the most excellent outdated laptops.

### 7.2 Cryptographic Applications:

Quantum figuring addresses a reasonable risk to current cryptographic strategies. To guard against future quantum attacks, researchers are looking into quantum-safe cryptography.

## 8. Biometrics and Facial Affirmation:

### 8.1 Overhauled Security endeavors:

In different applications, from cell phones to air terminal security, biometric confirmation strategies, for example, facial acknowledgment, unique mark filtering, and voice acknowledgment, give improved security to personality check.

8.2 Security Concerns:

Worries about the security of delicate individual information assortment and capacity are raised by the boundless utilization of biometrics. Finding a balance between convenience and privacy is still challenging.

## 9. RPA, or mechanical interaction robotization,:

9.1 Robotizing Tedious Tasks:

Via mechanizing monotonous and rule-based assignments with programming robots, RPA opens up HR for additional innovative and complex errands. It very well may be utilized in client assistance, HR, and money.

9.2 Reconciliation with AI-based computers:

Getting RPA together with man-made knowledge progressions updates computerization limits by enabling robots to conform to dynamic circumstances, choose, and gain from data.

## 10. Space Advancements and Examination:

10.1 Secret Space Examination:

SpaceX and Blue Beginning's contribution in space investigation is speeding up improvements in rocket innovation, satellite sending, and a potential future space the travel industry.

10.2 Supergroups of satellites and stars:

To give worldwide web inclusion, organizations are conveying gigantic heavenly bodies of satellites.

The computerized gap can be spanned and distant regions can be associated with this innovation.

As these developments mature, they will for certain reshape adventures, social orders, and how we speak with the world. Watch out for the continually changing advanced scene.

## Future Examples in Frameworks organization: Exploring the New Horizons

The field of systems administration is undergoing rapid change as a result of novel developments, shifting customer demands, and the increasing complexity of interconnected frameworks. There are various arising patterns that can possibly change organizing in the years to come. The following are a couple of basic examples to watch:

### 1. 5G Advancement Improvement:

1.1 Past Adaptable Associations:
While 5G initially gained a reputation for being unmistakable in the mobile sector, its impact is

spreading to other industries. Expect greater participating in regions like clinical consideration, gathering, and splendid metropolitan networks, opening extra open doors in accessibility and continuous applications.

1.2 Secretive 5G Businesses:

Affiliations are researching the sending of private 5G associations to meet express accessibility needs inside their premises. Assembling and coordinated operations, for instance, require high-data transmission, low-dormancy correspondence, so this pattern is particularly significant.

## 2. Edge Enlisting Compromise:

2.1 Appropriated Designing:

Edge enlisting conveys computational resources closer to the data source, decreasing inaction and working on ceaseless dealing with. This example is getting energy for applications requiring brief responses, as IoT, free vehicles, and extended reality.

2.2 Murkiness Enrolling:

Fog figuring, an increase of edge enrolling, incorporates dealing with data at various concentrations between the device and the cloud. This approach upgrades resource use and further creates capability in directing data streams.

## 3. Reason Based Frameworks organization (IBN):

3.1 Modernized Association The chiefs:

IBN includes networks that can consequently arrange and oversee gadgets as per undeniable level orders from heads. This shift towards automation further develops network adequacy, diminishes mix-ups, and engages faster response to advancing circumstances.

3.2 Self-Repair Businesses:
Networks with self-repairing limits utilize man-made insight and motorization to constantly recognize and determine issues. This reduces individual time, further creates steadfast quality, and limits the necessity for manual intervention in network support.

## 4. Reproduced insight Driven Association Security:

4.1 Lead Assessment:
Man-made knowledge driven security courses of action impact lead assessment to recognize anomalies and potential security risks. By identifying designs that

are indicative of digital threats, this proactive approach enhances network security.

4.2 Zero Trust Security Models:

Zero Trust plan, which anticipates that no component, whether inside or outside the association, can be depended upon obviously, is transforming into a standard for getting networks. This approach prevents equal advancement by requiring affirmation for every client and device attempting to get to resources.

## 5. Programming Portrayed Frameworks organization (SDN) and Association Capacity Virtualization (NFV):

5.1 Strong Association Coordination:

SDN and NFV continue to propel, offering dynamic association coordination and versatility. This example licenses relationship to change their association system rapidly to meet developing necessities, scaling resources dependent upon the situation.

5.2 Association Cutting:

With the progress of 5G, the possibility of association removing goes to be more obvious. This includes enhancing asset utilization and execution and creating virtualized, altered network sections tailored to specific applications or client groups.

## 6. Quantum Frameworks organization:

6.1 Quantum Key Scattering (QKD):

Quantum key circulation for secure correspondence is acquiring consideration as the field of quantum figuring creates. Another degree of cryptographic security is given by QKD, which scrambles correspondence channels by using quantum properties.

6.2 Quantum-Secure Correspondence Shows:

Research is ceaseless to encourage quantum-safe cryptographic shows that can get through potential risks from quantum laptops, ensuring the continued with security of association correspondences.

## 7. Hyperautomation:

7.1 Coordination of PC based knowledge and Automation:

Hyperautomation incorporates the wide use of man-made knowledge and motorization mechanical assemblies to grow human capacities. This converts into the computerized administration of complicated undertakings in systems administration, bringing about expanded efficiency and diminished functional expenses.

7.2 Investigation for Shrewd Organizations:

The game plan of clever association examination instruments, constrained by man-made insight, engages relationship to get further encounters into network execution, perceive bottlenecks, and seek after informed decisions to improve as a rule.

## 8. Conservative Frameworks organization:

8.1 Energy-Successful Structure:

With a creating focus on legitimacy, the frameworks organization industry is exploring energy-capable establishment and eco-obliging practices. This consolidates the improvement of low-power contraptions, propelling server ranch undertakings, and utilizing harmless to the ecosystem power sources.

8.2 Green Enrolling Practices: Affiliations are coordinating green figuring practices into their association systems, producing into account the regular results of association establishment and searching for approaches to restricting carbon impressions.

## 9. Propelling Organization Standards:

These standards are vital for supporting the creating number of related devices and the interest for high speed, reliable remote organization.

9.2 6G Examination: As 5G associations complete, assessment and examination concerning 6G advancement have recently begun. Expected to be open in the accompanying decade, 6G should give significantly faster paces, lower lethargy, and creative use cases past what 5G offers.

The combination of emerging innovations, clever robotization, enhanced security, and a dynamic and ground-breaking excursion are the distinguishing characteristics of the systems administration of the future. Staying up with the latest with these examples will be major for affiliations hoping to manufacture flexible, capable, and future-arranged network structures.

System administration terminology glossary A Passage (AP): A device that grants far off contraptions to communicate with a wired association using Wi-Fi.

Address Goal Convention, or ARP: Within a neighborhood organization, a convention is used to plan Macintosh IP locations.

Authentication: The most well-known approach to affirming the personality of a client, device, or structure.

B

Move speed: An organization's most extreme information move rate, ordinarily communicated in bits each second (bps).

Firewall: A security contraption or programming that screens and controls drawing closer and dynamic association traffic considering destined security rules.

Botnet: a group of compromised computers (bots) that are restricted by a central server and used for malicious activities.

C

Disseminated registering: The transport of enlisting organizations, including limit, dealing with, and programming, over the web.

DNS (Region Name System): a framework that changes over IP addresses into space names that can be perused by people.

Neighborhood, or LAN: a company that connects computers and other devices in a small area, like a home, office, or park.

D Dynamic Host Configuration Protocol: An association show that subsequently gives out IP areas to contraptions on an association.

DoS (Refusal of Organization): An attack that floods an association or structure with traffic to make it blocked off to clients.

Computerized Endorser Line, or DSL: an association with the web with a high velocity that utilizes the phone lines that are as of now set up.

E

Encryption: The strategy engaged with changing information into a protected code over totally to safeguard it from unapproved access.

Ethernet: A by and large used LAN development that uses a show to control how data groups are placed on the association.

Registering the edge: Taking care of data near the wellspring of data age as opposed to relying upon a concentrated cloud server.

F Bar: An association security system that screens and controls drawing nearer and dynamic association traffic considering predestined security rules.

FTP (Record Move Show): A standard association show used to move reports beginning with one host then onto the following over a TCP-based network, similar to the web.

G Access: a gadget that deciphers between different organization conventions and interfaces different organizations.

GPS (Overall Arranging System): a route framework that utilizations satellites to assist clients with pinpointing their definite area.

Hypertext Move Convention, or H HTTP: The preparation of data correspondence on the Web.

Hub: A fundamental frameworks organization device that partners different contraptions in a LAN anyway doesn't channel data.

I

IP Address (Web Show Address): a number that is given to every gadget that is a piece of a PC organization.

Web of Things, or IoT: The grouping of actual devices that have sensors, programming, and the ability to exchange information with other devices and frameworks over the internet.

J

Jitter: The assortment in package appearance times in an association, making misfortunes for data transmission.

K Spyware: Harmful programming that records keystrokes on a PC, getting fragile information like passwords.

L

Lethargy: The time concede between the subsequent data is sent and the subsequent it is gotten.

Load Balancer: A contraption or programming that similarly courses moving toward association traffic across various servers to prevent over-trouble.

M MAC Address, or Media Access Control Address: a stand-out identifier given to organize interfaces for use in network correspondence.

Malware: Malicious programming planned to naughtiness or exploit laptops or associations.

Network Association: a geography of the organization where every hub communicates information to the organization.

N

Network: A combination of laptops, servers, incorporated PCs, network contraptions, and various devices related with one another for sharing data and resources.

Network Show: a bunch of rules for the transmission of information over an organization.

Node: a computer, server, or other organizational device that serves as a place of association within an organization.

O

OSI Model (Open Systems Interconnection Model): A sensible framework used to sort out network collaborations, involving seven layers.

P Package: a piece of data sent across an organization.

Phishing: A sort of computerized attack where aggressors doubles into unveiling tricky information.

Administration's (QoS) Q nature: a collection of technologies that guarantee a certain level of performance for particular applications and control the network's resources.

R

Switch: An association contraption that progresses data between PC associations.

Ransomware: malicious software that makes a client's documents difficult to understand and demands payment in advance of their delivery.

S

Server: A PC or structure that directs network resources and offers sorts of help to various laptops, known as clients.

Subnet: a segment of an IP organization that is coherently divided.

T                TCP/IP (Web Convention/Transmission Control Convention): A set-up of correspondence shows used to interact devices on the web.

Diversion: Harmful programming covered as a real program that does unapproved exercises when ordered.

U

UDP (Client Datagram Show): A connection